Foundation for Educational Administration, Inc.
12 Centre Drive
Monroe Township, New Jersey 08831
Website: www.njpsa.org

International Standard Book Number 0-9788317-0-5

Cover design by Linda J. Walko

Printed in the United States of America

Acknowledgements

Over the years, countless people have encouraged me to explore the subject of discipline, to document my observations, and eventually to write this book. I give special thanks first, to my mentors and teachers: Dr. Joseph Yaeger, Dr. Linda Sommers, and Dr. Janet Emig. Thank you for your leadership, inspiration, and example.

I am especially grateful to the hundreds of teachers and administrators who opened their classrooms and schools to my work, who have tried and retried my suggestions to improve discipline in their schools, and who have enriched the CLICK program with their own ideas and feedback.

To the Boards of Directors of the New Jersey Principals and Supervisors Association and the Foundation for Educational Administration, I am grateful for your vision and support.

To JoAnn Bartoletti, an outstanding leader and example of integrity and commitment, thank you for being a guiding light and a true friend.

To my good friend, Art Firestone, I love your wit and wisdom, your passion and support.

To the entire staff of NJPSA/FEA , thanks for the good cheer when I needed it.

To Linda Walko, thank you for being efficient and helpful in seeing the manuscript through to publication.

To Sharon McCarthy and Denise Hecht, whose love and loyalty and knowledge inspired me to great accomplishment, I applaud you both. You have truly made a difference in my life.

Finally, to my wife, Belinda, my mom, my children, Carlo, Michael, Jamie and Louis and my two granddaughters, Natalie Rose, and Kylie, you are my strength. You are the miracles in my life!

And to the millions of children in this world...everything is possible!

"Nothing splendid has ever been achieved

except by those who dared believe that

something inside of them was superior to circumstance."

---- Bruce Barton

"Every man is an impossibility until he is born."

---- Ralph Waldo Emerson

This book is dedicated to the memory of my father

who was a perfect example of unconditional love and support.

click

click \\'klik\ *vb* [prob. imit.] *vt* (1581) *vi* To fit or agree exactly.

click \\'klik\ *vb* [prob. imit.] *vt* (1581) *vi* To function smoothly.

cli'que \ 'klēk, klik\ *n* [F] (1711) A group of people held together by common interests.

Table of Contents

Preface

*T*he relationship between teacher or administrator and student has always been a fragile one--when the relationship works, life is a joy; when the relationship falters, **life gets messy!**

The CLICK program deals primarily with positive and sensible interventions for correcting student behavior. Most of the interventions are preventive rather than remedial, and focus on cooperation through effective communication skills. Additionally, most of the specific procedures in the program are based on actual practices used by teachers and administrators in the field--practitioners who provided the models and behaviors from which CLICK has been developed.

Much of the theory contained in this resource manual is based on the latest research in cognitive psychology, developmental psychology, psycho-linguistics, psychotherapy, education, and neuro-linguistic programming. Only those classroom management strategies and interventions that are practical, successful, flexible, and tested have been included.

All things being equal, a successful classroom environment begins with solid classroom management techniques. Additionally, teachers must always provide effective and academically challenging instruction-- instruction that meets the needs, interests, and ability levels of each student. Finally, teachers and administrators must care about and love kids. These basic ingredients make for successful and positive classroom and school environments.

Introduction

*T*he CLICK program defines *discipline* as a partnership, a cooperative effort among administrators, teachers, students, and parents in a specific environment. It's a *partnership* because K-12 teachers and students should share in creating rules of behavior for individual classrooms. This is of particular importance, because a shared rule-making process offers students a sense of ownership and control. Discipline is *cooperative* because it involves a give-and-take relationship among everyone involved. Discipline is *specific* because each classroom is unique. Although the school may have some overarching rules about lateness or advocates zero tolerance for credible threats, each classroom needs its own simple set of rules that match the needs of a particular teacher and group of students.

Like most subjects, discipline has connected to it a list of myths that are perpetuated through time. Here is a list of several "myths in discipline." Teachers and administrators may recognize some of these:

MYTH One cannot learn to be an effective disciplinarian. It's an innate skill.
REALITY In fact teachers-- even those who have had difficulty dealing with disciplinary issues--can and do learn successful discipline and classroom management techniques.

MYTH Some students are unreachable and cannot be disciplined.
REALITY One of the major assumptions of the CLICK program is that all students have the resources to effect change in themselves. Yes, some students seem unreachable and unresponsive, but this is more likely a reflection of the limitation of the teacher or that of a specific method than an indication of the student's resistance. The CLICK Faculty Meeting is designed to expand the teachers' repertoire of disciplinary and classroom management techniques, giving them the tools to solve even the most severe discipline problems. The CLICK Faculty Meeting operates under two simple principles: First, if something doesn't work, try another approach. Second, to solve problems, it's wise to think creatively. That's good advice, because far too often in education, if something doesn't work we tend to do it harder, more often, or louder, and we tend to rely on traditional or comfortable solutions instead of thinking creatively about the problem.

MYTH If the instruction is interesting, a teacher will never have a discipline problem.

REALITY Interesting instruction helps considerably, but one cannot rely on this being a complete deterrent to behavior problems. Even with the best teacher, unless the classroom management system is in place, effective teaching and learning will not occur. Successful classroom management encompasses many positive characteristics, including rapport, trust clarity, momentum, attention, listening, direction, and discipline.

MYTH Some classes are better than others.
REALITY Perhaps there have been occasions when you've walked into the faculty room and heard someone say something like: "If you think this year's fourth grade class is bad, you haven't seen anything yet. Wait until you get this year's third grade." Unfortunately, people are influenced by this sort of thinking and, often unconsciously, develop negative expectations. It's very unfair to think of students this way and usually, it isn't correct.

MYTH The more experience you have, the better you are at establishing discipline.
REALITY A poor disciplinarian with 20 years' experience gives the same poor performance each year. Experience doesn't guarantee anything. There are first-year teachers who are fantastic at classroom management, and veteran teachers who consistently perform poorly.

MYTH Students should know how to behave properly, especially those in middle and high school.
REALITY In order to act "properly," one must be taught how to act. Students must have a mental model of what's right and what's wrong. They must understand the difference between appropriate and inappropriate behavior. They must grasp the concept of cause and effect, and they must understand the consequences of their behaviors. Teachers and administrators must realize that students with disorders (such as Attention Deficit Hyperactivity Disorder [ADHD], Oppositional Defiant Behavior [OD], Conduct Disorder [CD], etc.) may have a different logic system than they do, and may think about behavior in entirely different ways than other students do. In many cases, these students know the rules and how to act, but they often have difficulty in retrieving the rules or controlling their behavior. This is particularly true of students with ADHD. (More will be said about thinking errors in a later chapter.)

MYTH Students will respond to "old-fashioned power and authority."
REALITY Imposing your will and power on students causes resentment, which only decreases a student's ability to learn because of stress from the imposition. Teachers may have a very well-disciplined and quiet class, but that may be more about obedience than anything else. The key to all good discipline is trust and rapport, the basic building blocks of the CLICK program. Quite simply, students respond to teachers who care about them.

4

MYTH All students should be able to follow a list of rules for behavior.

REALITY Lists of rules are totally ineffective unless the rules are tied to teacher expectation. Additionally, rules only reflect behavioral considerations. To help ensure success, the CLICK program adds two essential and important ingredients for behavior change. First, in order to change a student's negative behavior to positive behavior, consideration must be given to the personality of the student. Second, in order to change behavior, consideration must be given to the negative or limiting beliefs of the student. Beliefs drive and influence behavior; to change a specific behavior, the belief must change first. (More will be said about these concepts later in the text.)

MYTH Students should always listen to you because you are the teacher or the administrator.

REALITY Students listen to teachers and administrators who listen to them. Listening is an attitude, not a skill. A positive attitude goes a long way in building relationships with others. Mark Twain said, "You have two ears and a mouth." That should be a clue. The CLICK program stresses listening as high on the list of needs for most students.

In order to be effective disciplinarians, teachers and administrators need to act based on realities rather than myths. The CLICK program is intended to arm educators with the skills, knowledge, and dispositions required for effective discipline.

Chapter 1

How To Create a Positive Classroom Environment

*E*ffective classroom managers apply some very basic principles to create classroom environments that nurture and support social-emotional development and learning for all students. These key principles are briefly discussed in this chapter and addressed further in later chapters.

Principle 1
Apply the Law of Requisite Variety

To paraphrase Ashby's Law of Requisite Variety,[1] a person within a system with the most flexibility usually has the most control. In other words, flexibility is the key to good discipline. Simply put, if something doesn't work, do something else.

The key to good discipline is to prevent misbehavior from recurring, and not encouraging it to occur over and over again. Visit most detention rooms or classroom time-out areas, and you'll see many of the same students on a regular basis. Discipline has become institutionalized and routine; when that happens, it is ineffective. Incidentally, one of the saddest results of school detention is that, when students are asked why they are in detention, they quite often respond, "I don't know." And most times, they sincerely don't because there is little or no connection between what they did and their time in detention.

Principle 2
Avoid quick-fix solutions

If a teacher is too quick to assign detention, keeps students after school, sends students out of the classroom for every little infraction, or randomly doles out punishment without thinking through the why's and what for's, trouble will most likely follow. Teachers, administrators, parents, and students need to talk about the classroom management plan on a regular basis, or consistency and effectiveness will be lost.

---

[1] Ashby, W., *An Introduction to Cybernetics,* Wiley, (1957)

Discipline is everybody's business! One of the most powerful methods for achieving consistency and a shared vision about discipline is the CLICK Faculty Meeting, which is discussed in chapter five of this resource manual. Another way is to form a team of interested parents, community members, teachers, students, and support staff to regularly review discipline policies, take school climate surveys, and interview staff and students about the school environment.[2]

Principle 3
Be fair and flexible

Each student is unique and is motivated differently. A one-size-fits-all policy results in a system that's unfair and ineffective. There needs to be an overriding and uniform structure in place. Unfortunately, most schools rely solely on a traditional discipline structure--teacher warnings, teacher-assigned detentions, calls home, parent conferences, suspensions, and expulsions. These strategies work for some students, particularly those student with minor infractions. However, there are students who do not respond to these forms of discipline at all; they are often noncompliant, disruptive, or even violent. These students need special programs and specially designed interventions.[3]

Teachers and administrators often talk about applying discipline equally; that, too, rarely works. Flexibility is everything. Equal or uniform discipline is the equivalent of 20 people going to the doctor with somewhat similar ailments and all receiving exactly the same treatment. A good doctor considers the individual patient, variations in symptoms, each patient's history, and other factors before making a diagnosis and recommending treatment. Teachers must be good diagnosticians. This is a skill that develops with experience, but it starts with using good tools and continuously monitoring and evaluating the students. Good classroom managers often talk to their students and get their opinions about what is working and what is not in terms of classroom discipline.

Principle 4
Make rules that
make sense

Sometimes in our anger or frustration, we say things we don't mean. "You are staying after school for five weeks straight" is ridiculous. Classroom rules and consequences must be discussed and planned in advance with students. Rules must be connected to expectations---and consequences---that have been clearly stated.[4]

---

[2] Blankstein, A., *Lessons for Life: How Smart Schools Boost Academic, Social, and Emotional Intelligence*, (2003). In M. J. Elias, H Arnold, and C., Stieger-Hussey (Ed.Ds.).*EQ & IQ: Best Leadership Practices for Caring and Successful Schools*, Thousand Oaks, CA, Corwin Press

[3] Levy, Ray and O'Hanlon, Bill, *Try and Make Me: Simple Strategies That Turn Off the Tantrums and Create Cooperation,* Rodale Inc.

[4] Payne, Ruby K., *A Framework for Understanding Poverty* (Third Revised Edition), Aha! Process, Inc. (2003)

Principal 5
Model the behavior
that you want

For example, if you have a rule that directs the students to raise their hand before speaking, you might say to the students, "I would like someone to answer question six in the book." and, as you say this, have your hand raised to model what a student should do. If you make a rule that students must walk quietly to assembly programs, then as you walk with them through the corridors, you should be quiet also. Modeling behaviors you expect is a key element in teaching proper behavior.[5]

Principal 6
Hold students
accountable

Accountability is a sign of respect. Expect students to tell the truth; teach them not to blame others and to be responsible for their own behavior. Try to foster self-discipline and a sense of responsibility for their own actions. Teach your students honesty and courage. Help them to understand that when they do something wrong, they must be prepared to face the consequences.

Principal 7
Engage your
students

Create the optimal classroom environment, both physically and emotionally. At minimum, making your activities brief---even at the high school level---helps students who have attention problems. Always choose high-interest activities whenever possible, and remember to segment your instruction---chunking information into groups of three or four so students can remember information better. If possible, vary the environment: Set up learning centers and different kinds of grouping patterns and other physical alternatives. Familiarize yourself with and use brain-compatible teaching strategies. Remember to plan activities that use at least two of the three learning modalities---visual, auditory, and kinesthetic as part of your instructional delivery. Finally, pre-assess and assess on a regular basis.[6]

---

[5] DePorter, Bobbi with Hernacki, Mike, *Quantum Learning,* Dell Publishing, (1992)
[6] Jensen, E., *Brain-Based Learning,* 2nd Edition, san Diego, CA, The Brain Store (2000)
Sousa, D., *How the Brain Learns: A Classroom Teacher's Guide*, 2nd Edition, Thousand Oaks, CA, (2001)

Chapter 2

What Are the Skills of Effective Classroom Managers?

To be successful as a teacher, one's classroom management skills must be finely tuned. Teachers who are effective classroom managers share a number of common characteristics, traits, and skills that can be easily learned. Following are the skills that lead to good classroom management.

Skill 1
Develop good rapport and trust with all of their students

For example, one teacher had a student suspended for serious misbehavior. When the student returned to class, the teacher was waiting for him at the classroom door. The teacher smiled, happily greeted him and said, "I know we had a problem; let's see it we both can put our differences behind us. Welcome back!" Now *that's* rapport building. An undesirable alternative would be to greet the returning student with a warning to "take your seat and start behaving a little better or more suspensions will be in your future." Instead, this teacher did the opposite, gaining the student's trust and building rapport.

Building rapport and gaining trust are learnable skills.[7] They are the basic building blocks of all relationships.[8]

Skill 2
Emphasize prevention and planning

Effective teachers are proactive. They have a keen ability to anticipate where things can go awry, and plan their day so the class will run smoothly. Here's an example of what I'm talking about: A student suddenly bursts into the room, late for class and obviously angry about something that just happened outside the classroom. The teacher notices the anger---the student is gritting his teeth, his fists are closed, and he throws his book down hard on his desk. The teacher calmly but briskly

---

[7] Costa, A., and Garmston, R., *Cognitive Coaching*, Norwood, MA Christopher-Gordon Publishers (1994)
[8] Bandler, R. and Grinder, J., *The Structure of Magic* Palo Alto, CA Science and Behavior Books, Inc. (1975)

walks over to the student, bends down, and quietly says, " You are obviously upset. That's okay. You just sit there and relax if you can, and when you're ready, you can join the class. Just make sure you don't bother anyone. As a matter of fact, you don't have to do anything. Just sit calmly." This is a preventative action. If the teacher had reacted by demanding that the student get to work immediately, it would probably infuriate and distance the student further.

Skill 3
Keep students' attention

Keep the attention of all students with interesting tasks, momentum, and easy transitions. Keeping a good pace or rhythm in teaching helps greatly with discipline, particularly when teaching students who have attention problems. Lessons that begin in a novel way (the brain loves things new and different) capture student attention. Variety, short tasks, and group work help to maintain this attention. Finally, easy simple routines and transitions sustain this momentum. Sample lesson plans that illustrate these strategies and help you meet the criteria of good teaching, in general, are provided later.

Skill 4
Maintain a full view of all of their students

It is important that the teacher has a full view of each student and is able to scan the room and establish full eye contact with every student. If students have any ideas about throwing objects, hitting their neighbors, shouting, or creating more subtle disruptions, having a full view of the classroom lets the teacher spot these behaviors before they begin---or just as they occur. Regardless of the specific seating arrangements, teachers must be able to move easily in and out of the aisles, from the front of the room to the back. Because it's a good way to keep students on task, all good classroom managers move about the room on a regular basis.

Skill 5
Redirect misbehavior

Effective classroom managers skillfully redirect students' behaviors. For example, a teacher turned during a lesson and noticed a girl writing her name on her desk. The teacher simply said, "What should you be doing?" The girl responded, "My math problems." If the teacher had said, "What are you doing?" the response may have been, "I'm writing my name on the desk. Can't you see?" In the first instance, the teacher redirected the student's thinking; in the second, the teacher was opening the door for trouble.

Skill 6
Treat students with respect

The best way to redirect behavior is through effective use of language. Listed in the appendix are language patterns that teachers may find useful in dealing with everyday problems (e.g., keeping students on task, diffusing anger, containing arguments).

One rule of thumb in the CLICK program is never to scream, yell or publicly embarrass a student. The goal is to remain calm at all times.

Skill 7
Be caring, fair and equitable

Good classroom managers send a message to their students both verbally and non verbally---a message of caring. When students feel you care about them, rapport and trust are increased. Through your actions and language, let them know you want them to succeed, you believe in them, and you will never give up on them. When students trust you and are convinced you care, misbehavior decreases greatly. Trust and rapport form the foundation for all good relatinships.[9]

Skill 8
Know how to set clear expectations and limits for student behavior

Expectations set the framework for behavior in a classroom and for building classroom rules with students. For example, a teacher may set three major expectations for her students: safety, responsibility, and respect. The students and the teacher then create rules that are based on these three expectations. This limits the number of rules for the classroom to three or four and thus makes it easier for students to remember the rules. Part of chapter three is devoted to rules and expectations.

Skill 9
Know when to set limits for openly defiant students

The following are examples of how to deal with defiant students. They are based on the One-Word Discipline program.[10] Example 1 illustrates what happens when a teacher is not in control of a situation and lets the student direct the conversation and the outcome. Example 2 shows how to properly set limits.

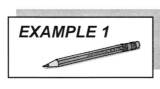
EXAMPLE 1

Student (Getting out of his seat):	"I need to see my guidance counselor now so I can change my math class."
Teacher:	"In the middle of everything, you have to see your counselor? I don't think so."
Student:	"Why? This is important to me. I have to change my class."
Teacher:	"Well, this class is important, too. Sit in your sear!"
Student:	"That's not fair. You let other kids out of here for other things!"
Teacher:	"I don't let other kids out of here, and you're no exception."
Student:	"I suppose you never had an emergency and had to go somewhere in the middle of something."

---

[9] Kohn, Alfie, *Beyond Discipline: From Compliance to Community,* Association for Supervision and Curriculum Development, Alexandria, VA, ASCD Publishers (1996)
[10] Bodenhammer, Gregory, *Back In Control: How To Get Children To Behave,* Fireside, New York, NY (1992)

This scene might not have happened if the teacher knew how to set limits. Let's change the scene a little and give you an idea of a strategy that works well in this kind of situation. In this scenario the teacher sets limits through the use of one key word. Notice the changes in language patterns and the use of one key word. (Important passages are underlined.)

The student starts to get out of his seat, and the dialogue begins the way it did in the previous passage.

Student:	"I need to see my guidance counselor now so I can change my math class."
Teacher:	"<u>Regardless</u> of what you have to do, please sit in your seat now."
Student:	"Why? This is important to me. I have to change my class!"
Teacher:	"<u>Regardless</u> of what you have to do and what is or is not important, sit in your seat."
Student:	"That's not fair. You let other kids out of the class for other things!"
Teacher:	"<u>Regardless</u> if this is fair or not, I want you to sit down now."
Student:	"I can't stand that word, regardless!"
Teacher:	"<u>Nevertheless</u>, sit down now."

In the first scene, the student has full control of the situation and leads the teacher in the conversation by simply changing the subject repeatedly. Students are expert in changing the subject,

In the second case, the teacher retains full control and does not get pulled into the student's arguments. The teacher puts up a verbal wall ("regardless" or "nevertheless") that the student cannot penetrate. This is called the One-Word Discipline Program.

Here is another example of the One-Word Discipline Program in practice.

EXAMPLE 2

Student:	"Teacher, teacher, may I sharpen my pencil?"
Teacher:	"No, you may not."
Student:	"Please, all the teachers let us sharpen our pencils."
Teacher:	"<u>Regardless</u> of what other teachers do, the rule is no sharpening pencils after the bell."
Student:	"That's not fair."

Teacher:	"<u>Regardless</u> of whether it is fair or not, the rule still stands."
Student:	"I don't believe you! It's not a big deal!"
Teacher:	"<u>Regardless</u> of whether it's a big deal or not, the deal is that we pay attention to our agreed upon rules."

Skill 10

Anticipate and think through the effect that consequences might have on student behavior

There are two important questions that effective classroom managers ask themselves in delivering consequences:

(1) What effect will the consequences have in changing the behavior of the student?

(2) What is the probability that this negative behavior will not happen again as a result of the consequence?

For example, if a student purposely throws papers on the floor, the consequence should be to clean up the mess. If a student is late to class, the student should make up the exact time and the missed work after class or school. In many classrooms, however, if a student throws papers on the floor or is late for class, a teacher assigns detention. There is no connection between the offense and the punishment. More important than the punishment is a discussion between the teacher and the student about the behavior, especially if the assigned consequence does not work or stop the unwanted behavior.

Skill 11

Know students well and detect early signs of behavior problems

Effective classroom managers use a system that allows for early detection of students who may have behavior problems. The CLICK Survey, [11] which appears in Chapter Six, was developed to help educators accurately predict students' personality and behavioral tendencies. Students who are extreme in any of these personality styles can create discipline problems.

---

[11] Hecht, D., *The Quick CLICK Survey*, New Jersey Principals and Supervisors Association, (1996)

Chapter 3

The First Weeks of School

The teacher's first order of business for the first few weeks of school is building relationships with students. Most of the school year will be devoted to substantive work, but building relationships and establishing routines are the first two orders of business. Also, there is no reason why continued relationship building cannot be combined with subject work throughout the year.

Learning involves two things: task and relationship.[12] *Task* is content or the *what* of teaching and learning. Teachers generally know what to teach their students; the problem is *how* to teach them. Educators are finding it increasingly difficult to know how to teach and reach today's students. It's difficult to pinpoint which of today's many influences create students whom educators find difficult to teach. However, positive classroom relationships seem to have the most bearing on positive student behavior. As a matter of fact, the one factor that seems to have the most positive impact on student achievement is the quality of the relationships that exist in the school, especially inside the classroom. Relationship is the key to everything.

There are four guiding principles that help to improve relationship between the teachers and the students. [13]

1. When communicating with students, the behavioral response that you get is the real meaning or result of the communication, regardless of what you intended it to be. Communication involves a lot more than talking. It also includes sensory acuity and attentive listening.
2. No matter the verbal response, the student's behavioral response represents the best choice or response the student can give for that

---

[12] Dilts, R., *Dynamic Learning*, Meta Publications, Capitola, CA (1995)
[13] Dilts, R., *Applications of Neuro-Linguistic Programming: A Practice to Communications Learning and Change,* Meta Publications, Capitola, CA (1983)

situation at that time. A student's behavior demonstrates the student's flexibility and the alternatives known to him or her at that time. A teacher may not approve of that particular behavior and may even think the behavior is immature or silly, but that is the choice the student has made. If a teacher wants a student's behavior to change, the teacher must teach new choices.

3. There is no such thing as failure, only feedback. That is to say, one doesn't fail; one has just discovered what one didn't know. When failure is viewed as an opportunity to learn rather than a signal to give up or to place blame, students can grow. Conversely, in order for students to learn and flourish, teachers must create a risk-free environment.

4. In order for a person to change a behavior, three conditions are usually necessary: (a) the person must know how to change; (b) the person must want to change; (c) the person must have the opportunity to change. Therefore, the teacher has the responsibility to teach behavior skills; the teacher must be familiar with a student's highest values to motivate the student to change; and the teacher must provide enough time for the change to occur.

The First Day and Beyond...

On the first day of school, cheerfully meet the students at the door and seat them in an orderly fashion. Put your name on the board, and have the students participate in an activity that allows them to provide you with information about themselves. For preschoolers or kindergarteners, this might be some sort of oral activity. Students who are in second grade or higher might fill out information cards. Make sure you have arranged the desks or tables beforehand for the student's arrival. Seating charts are highly recommended.

After gathering information about the students, use a suggested icebreaker to start the rapport-building process. Each of the CLICK Icebreakers has critical-thinking skills embedded in them and can start students on the road to thinking critically. Research indicates that disruptive students lack critical-thinking skills.[14] Students who think logically and critically have fewer discipline and personal problems.[15] For example, Icebreaker 1, involves the skills of speaking, listening attentively, synthesizing and organizing information, and drawing conclusions. These skills are built into each of the CLICK Icebreakers. After getting to know your students through simple discussions and icebreakers, you will be able to introduce rules and expectations, possibly on the second or third day.

---

[14] Fuerstein, Reuven, *Instrumental Enrichment: An Intervention Program for Cognitive Modifiability,* Scott Foresman and Co., Glenville, IL (1980)

[15] Shure, Myrna, Ph.D., *Raising a Thinking Child,* Simon and Schuster Inc. (1994)

Throughout the first week, continue the ice-breakers, set up rules and regulations, build rapport and trust among the students, review expectations, and call the parents of those few students you suspect may need special attention before there is an actual problem. Explain to the parents that you want to help. Ask them for advice; assure them that you are there for them and their child and will involve them in your plans at every turn. Ideally, you should devote about 25% of each day to building rapport and establishing rules and regulations.

Display a copy of the finalized classroom rules, placing them strategically where the students can see them from anywhere in the classroom. Students should be given copies of the rules to share with their families. A copy should also be given to the school principal, who should collect and distribute the rules from every classroom so they can be used for a faculty discussion during the first full faculty meeting. Such a discussion of all the rules builds consistency among staff members and ensures that none of the classroom rules are in direct conflict with another rule or with the school district's policy. This discussion can also provide an opportunity to improve, modify, or eliminate problematic rules. All rules should be aligned with and help to contribute to the accomplishment of the school 's mission.

Ice-Breakers for the First Two Weeks of School

A primary reason for using ice breakers in the first week or two of school is to give students a chance to open up to each other and to develop respect for each other on a deeper level. Ice breakers also provide an excellent way to strengthen rapport among your students and, in some cases and depending on the icebreaker, they can help students develop their listening, speaking, organizing, and synthesizing skills. As mentioned previously, one of the reasons why developing thinking skills is important is that children who think critically tend to have fewer discipline problems. Myrna Shure's book, *Raising a Thinking Child,* is an excellent source for helping children learn to think critically and for teaching children good from bad, right from wrong, cause and effect, actions and consequences, and other important concepts. Children who don't have these skills are very often thoughtless when reacting to others in problem areas.

Ice-Breaker 1:

Student **A** talks to Student **B** for two minutes. Student **B** just listens attentively. Student **A** tells something original or interesting about himself/herself. No dialogue is allowed. While listening to Student **A**,

Student **B** makes up a book or a movie title to capture the essence of that person. Call time after two minutes and ask for volunteers to reveal the book title they came up with and why they chose that particular title. Have the students change roles and repeat the exercise.

Ice-Breaker 2:

Seat Students in a circle and have them complete the following phrases:
- My biggest fear is...
- My best dream is...
- My best vacation was...
- My most embarrassing moment was...

Ice-Breaker 3:

Have students interview each other using a tape recorder. (Note taking will suffice where tape recorders are not available.) Four questions are asked:
- If you could be an animal, what animal would you be?
- If you could be famous for something, what would that be?
- What kind of friend do you want and why?
- If you could design a T-Shirt that represents what you are all about, what would it look like?

Ice-Breaker 4:

Have students bring photographs from home to class. Limit the photos to about 10. Have students tell about each photo (in small groups).

Ice-Breaker 5:

Have each student write 10 characteristics that describe her/himself. For example: I am creative; I like chocolate; I love the beach. Students do not put their names on the lists. Take the lists and place them on the floor in the center of the room. The teacher (or selected students) reads the lists and tries to identify the person based on the characteristics.

Ice-Breaker 6:

Have a scavenger hunt. After the scavenger hunt is completed, tell the students to explain their particular strategies for finding things. Then, ask how they can use their strategies elsewhere, including in the classroom.

Ice-Breaker 7:

What if...How come... I wonder why... These are the questions to answer in small groups. For example: What if people could fly? How come people get angry? Why does the ocean have waves?

Ice breaker 8:

Organize "it really bugs me" circles. Have groups of five students each list their gripes. Ask them to select gripes that apply to disciplinary problems in school or class. For example: "It really bugs me that we have to start school so early in the morning."

Ice-Breaker 9:

Ask the students to answer the following questions:

- If you could invite any five famous people to dinner tonight, who would they be? Why did you choose them?
- What would the seating be like?
- How do you think the conversation would progress?
- How do you think they would get along?
- What do you think you would serve them for dinner?
- What friends would you invite, and why?

SETTING CLASSROOM RULES

Good rules should be specific enough to avoid many misinterpretations. Good rules are reasonable, make sense, and tell students what to do. For example, "Don't run" doesn't tell students what to do; it just tells them *one thing* not to do. Additionally, good rules are modeled by the teacher and have a basic expectation tied to them. Finally, good rules are reinforced and repeated continuously by the teacher in both word and practice.[16]

As far as *school-wide rules* are concerned, only two are necessary.* These are:

> **Rule I:** Respect all people and property.
> **Rule II:** Listen to all staff members in the school.

These two rules will cover just about every major behavior infraction. To have 50 or 60 rules for students to remember is ludicrous. Take these two rules and discuss them with the students in an assembly program, in the classroom, or both. Explain what each means and give plenty of examples. If the school chooses to discuss the rule during an assembly, teachers can have follow-up discussions in their own classrooms. Remember, rules should tell students what they can do as well as what they can't do. Students should also know they can appeal rules they feel are not fair, but this must be done in the proper way. Familiarize students with the appeal process. Problems are less likely to occur when students are involved from the beginning in developing classroom rules.

---

[16] Saphier, Jon and Grower, Robert, *The Skillful Teacher*, 5th Edition, Research for Better Teaching, Inc., Carlisle, MA (1997)

*Note: In light of today's climate, teachers and administrators might want to add the following school wide rule: Report any violent, unusual or threatening behavior.

Discussion Questions for Building Rules

It's best to work with the students to develop classroom rules. The following discussion questions will help you begin your classroom discussions on rules and consequences. Remember to limit your classroom rules to about five or six (even fewer for young students). When there are too many rules, students who have attention problems will have difficulty remembering and retrieving them all.

Discussion questions:

- What is a good student?
- What is a good classroom?
- What is a good teacher?
- What are the responsibilities of students and of teachers?
- How can parents get involved in discipline?
- What are acceptable student behaviors?
- What are some consequences?
- What is fair?

Tie Rules to Expectations

It's best to tie or connect your rules to your expectations. For example, say to the students, "I expect this classroom to be a safe one; I expect you to be productive and do your class work and homework at all times; and I expect you to respect one another." Next, explain what safety, productivity, and respect are. Make sure *all* the students understand specifically what you mean by your expectations.

Next, divide the students into groups of three and have them create one or two rules for each of the expectations. Then select the three best rules and have these rules become the guiding behaviors for the class. For a rule of safety, one elementary student wrote the following: "Use your mouth for speaking politely and asking for things you need, and your hands and feet for helping."

Safety, respecting others, and being productive are three good expectations that cover most behaviors in a classroom. Other expectations may be caring, responsibility, sharing, and being polite, but remember to limit the number to about three.

Examples of Good Rules

- Treat each other with kindness and respect.
- Follow the teacher's requests.
- Listen to the teacher and others when they speak.
- Be prepared each day with whatever is required: notebook, pen, homework, textbook, et cetera.
- Respect each another's property.
- Check with the teacher when you can't solve a problem yourself.

Notice that all of these rules are positive and tell students what to do as opposed to what not to do.

The Values Triangle

Einstein once said you can't solve a problem on the same level that it occurs. If a teacher applies this statement to the behavior of students, it makes all the sense in the world. Experience tells us, behavior modification is the least effective method for effecting behavioral change because it tries to change behavior on a behavioral level.

Really good teachers—those who have few discipline problems—believe that working with an agreed upon set of values and beliefs results in faster, longer lasting behavioral change. To illustrate this, CLICK has developed what it calls the Values Triangle.[17] It works like this:

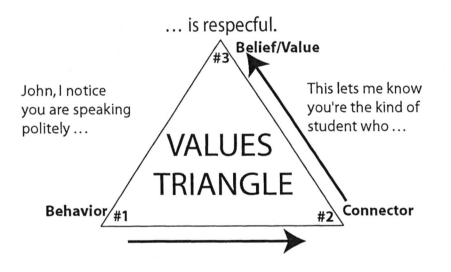

First, determine what your expectations are for your students. Using the example given previously, let us say you expect your students to be respectful. Every time you notice a particular student behaving in a respectful manner, say, "John, I noticed that you are speaking politely to your peers today; that lets me know you are being respectful."

In this way, the teacher connects expectation (value) to a behavior (speaking politely), and reinforces the behavior by tying it to the expectation. This method helps students learn clearly what each word means through action as well as word, rather than just word. It also elevates the learning to a value level and, through continuous connections between the behavior and the value, helps students form an imprint of this

---

[17] Blackerby, D., *Rediscover the Joy of Leading*, Success Skills, Inc., Oklahoma City, OK (1996)

behavior in their minds. In this way, the idea of acting respectfully becomes a reality.

School Rules and the Law

A number of factors increase the likelihood that students will follow classroom rules. When discussing acceptable classroom and school behavior, it's important that students first realize they absolutely cannot do certain things because, if they do, they could be violating the law. Students should know, in a developmentally appropriate manner, the basic "facts of law" and the implications of violating these basic laws. They should understand that it is against the law to violate the rights of the majority, specifically involving:

- Health
- Property loss or damage
- Disruption of the learning environment
- Educational purpose

In his book *Judicious Discipline*, Forest Gathercool (1993) discusses a concept called "compelling constitutional rights." For example, every individual in this country has the right to an education. If another individual violates this right, he or she is infringing upon the other's constitutional rights. Similarly, one cannot seriously impair another's health or safety; nor can one cause property loss or damage to another.

Gathercool also states that the major advantage of presenting a shared knowledge of these concepts is that doing so prevents the onus from always falling on the teacher when he or she enforces certain rules related to school and legal policies. It is easier to draw this legal picture for both parents and students at the onset of each school year, so that the entire school community understands what can and cannot be done legally.

Chapter 4

The CLICK Strategies to Eliminate Misbehavior

*H*ere is a list of strategies that may help in particularly difficult or sensitive situations. Although there are no foolproof techniques or strategies that work in all instances, there are strategies that often stop misbehavior. Remember, if something doesn't work, try something else immediately. The following guidelines and lists contain strategies to use with confrontational students, and are intended to be used as a teacher wishes. Not every suggestion will work in a particular school or circumstance.

General Guide for Handling Confrontation

- Look for nonverbal cues (facial expressions, posture, body movements, etc.) that may indicate trouble is brewing.

- Get closer to the student, but be aware of how close you are. Pay attention to the student's nonverbal cues, and back off when the student's cues indicate that he or she is getting uncomfortable.

- Change the tone of your voice or the rate of your speech.

- Stop talking and wait.

- Pause for five seconds and get eye contact (if doing so is culturally appropriate); add gestures for redirection.

- Remind students of rules before the rules are broken (e.g., "Raise your hands before you speak."

- Remind the student of the rules. If misbehavior continues, give the student a choice to either stop the misbehavior or "suffer the consequences."

- Move the student to another location in the room, such as a time-out area.

⯈ Move the student to a preplanned or specific area where he or she can be supervised.

⯈ Remember to always show self-control and remain calm. When a student has successfully redirected, always praise him or her.

Difficult or sensitive situations vary. This is not a list of strategies that always apply to a fight, rude behavior, or a rule infraction. This is a list teachers might review and add to from time to time as a reminder of possible techniques.

When a Student Becomes Confrontational

Sooner or later, a teacher will be confronted by an angry student. When this occurs, there are a few simple steps you can take to ease or diffuse the situation. Above all, never argue with a student, especially in public. When you do, you lose. It will only cause embarrassment, resentment, and anger. Besides, it isn't necessary. If you really get stuck and don't know what to do, stand there in silence, if possible, until the student leaves, and then immediately contact an administrator to send for the student.

An important note: The guidelines provided below will work for 95% of the confrontations a teacher may experience over a period of years. For those very few students—especially older, larger students—who show signs of becoming violent, the teacher should have a way to get help. In light of recent violence, many schools now have protocols for getting in-school or law enforcement help when a student exhibits clear signs of imminent violence.

The following guidelines will help during an uneasy interaction with a student:

⯈ Be assertive and show confidence.

⯈ Clearly communicate to the student the behavior you expect of that student. Get close to the student (but do not invade his or her space), and reiterate the behavior you want; for example, "Return to your class immediately."

⯈ Be congruent in body posture, tone of voice, rate of speech, eye contact, and directions.

⯈ If it's culturally appropriate, make eye contact at the eye level of the student; kneel, if necessary, for younger students. (Note that this behavior is not always culturally appropriate. In some cultures, looking a person in the eye is disrespectful. With this in mind, it's important to have an informed understanding of the various cultures represented by your students, particularly with respect to actions and gestures that may be deemed inappropriate or offensive by a particular culture.) Stand almost sideways to the student, never face to face. Be sure that the student sees your hands at all times, and that you can see the student's hands as well, in case he or she is holding a weapon.

+ Match the intensity of the student's voice. Don't shout or speak softly. Keep your voice rhythmical, fluent, and firm.

+ Have some kind of signal system to notify colleagues of the status of the confrontation. For example, holding out one finger means "I'm okay." Holding out two fingers means "Stick around, something may happen." Holding out three fingers means "I need assistance now."

+ Never argue with a student, especially one who begins to raise his or her voice. Simply walk away (if you are a teacher) and get assistance. Remember the student's face for identification purposes. (Administrators, of course, should not walk away; a totally different strategy must be used.)

It's a good idea to discuss other possibilities for dealing with confrontational students at grade-level and faculty meetings. Remember, these are only general guidelines.

Highly Defiant Student

Some students are argumentative, critical, aggressive, and hostile. Some may be outright intimidating and abusive. Students who are highly defiant are usually very difficult to communicate with, and it's also usually hard to develop a rapport with these students.

Remember, these students are behaving in the only way that they know . Teachers and administrators need to believe and understand this if they are going to make any headway with them. In many instances, these students are victims of abuse themselves. Many lack coping skills, and often they are generally undisciplined. Some are on drugs. At worst, they are power-oriented and prone to violence. The following are some suggestions to remedy the negative behavior of highly defiant students.

+ Many defiant students respond to mentors and positive role models. Defiant students need to be taught reasonable behavior because they only know how to be aggressive or passive. In other words, they will either fight or flee. They don't know the in-between behavior of appropriate assertiveness.

+ Give defiant students a forum for venting their hostility. Special sessions can be set aside during or after the school day for them to talk and work through moral and social dilemmas, to complete special exercises on solving problems, and to share real stories in their lives.

This is not detention; it is special help, and students should know that the counselors and teachers involved are there to assist them. These students need help and guidance in making good decisions and thinking critically, because they very often work from a mental model that is very different from that of most people. For these students, things that make sense to us often don't make sense to them.[18]

◆ Conduct focus groups to discuss problems. For example, if two or three students have been unruly during lunch, the assistant principal, counselor, or another staff member might run a focus group during lunch. For a 40-minute lunch period, as an example, the students report to a special room instead of the lunchroom (they brown bag lunch). There, they eat for 20 minutes, and the remainder of the period is spent with the assistant principal discussing proper behavior during lunch. Discussing means give and take—not a lecture from an authority figure. The objective is for the students and the focus group leader to determine what some of the problems are and how they might be resolved. This is done each day until the assistant principal thinks the student can return to normal lunch. Focus groups can be run for any type of infraction, but the number in the group should be limited to no more than 10 students.

◆ Whenever possible, involve the parents of these students in all aspects of their school life. Suggest to the parents that they limit their children's exposure to violence, including violence in television, music, magazines, and comic books.[19]

◆ Use the CLICK Survey to identify the values and beliefs that these students possess, and connect them to consequences and ways to motivate the students. One suggestion that frequently works is to be firm and politely strict in your dealings with students. Never openly confront or challenge students who are defiant. Instead, diffuse the situation by saying something like, "I can't stand and argue, let's sit down and let's argue." Distraction techniques work well with students who are highly defiant, as does putting them in charge of an activity. The main thing to remember is that you must establish rapport and trust with them first of all. If that happens, much of their hostility will disappear.

◆ If and when a student is removed from a classroom, send the student to a time-out room rather than to the school office. If a student is not responding to a request to settle down, ask the student to go to time-out. In an elementary school, the time-out area could be as simple as

---

[18]Scannella, A. and Webster-O'Dell, Wendi (EDs.), *The Children We Share*, the Foundation for Educational Administration and the New Jersey Principals and Supervisors Association, Monroe Twp., NJ, funded by the New Jersey Department of Education (2003).
[19]Ibid.

an empty chair in the back of a neighboring classroom. In such a case, the student is directed to that chair and sits there quietly until the teacher comes for him or her. The teacher then deals with the misbehavior. Of course, the teachers have already explained a time-out to their students on the first day of school, so they understand the purpose and meaning of this procedure. Students need to know that time-out is an opportunity for them to calm down and get away from a difficult situation. It is not punishment. The students know that when they are sent to another teacher's classroom for a time-out, they will automatically meet with their own teacher after class or school. If the student does not report or meet with the teacher, the teacher should notify the assistant principal or principal, who will call the student's parent or guardian.

Discipline Checklist

Use the following checklist as a guideline for the minimum requirements for good classroom management and as a starting point for group discussions among teachers, students, and administrators.

- ☑ Do I smile frequently, and speak calmly most of the time?
- ☑ Have I developed a good rapport with my students? Did I neglect anyone?
- ☑ Do I pay attention to the "quiet" student?
- ☑ Have I taken more time to establish rapport and trust with the students who are more difficult to deal with?
- ☑ Have I allowed enough student participation in developing classroom rules? Should I do more?
- ☑ Are my rules and consequences clear and specific? Are they stated in the positive? Do the rules tell students what to do as opposed to what not to do?
- ☑ Do the consequences make sense? Have my students helped in formulating the consequences?
- ☑ Do the students think I am fair?
- ☑ Are my rules tied to my expectations?
- ☑ Do I connect rules to my expectations in the Values Triangle?
- ☑ Are my expectations and standards high but reachable?
- ☑ Do I hold students accountable for their actions? Have I taught my students that no really means no?

☑ Do I acknowledge my students' good behaviors and achievements regularly?

☑ Do I model behaviors I expect?

☑ Have I provided for all cultures and for diversity?

☑ Have I checked to see if any student has a physical or mental disability?

☑ Do I have enough information about all my students, particularly the students who seem to be difficult or resistant?

☑ Have I communicated with and contacted parents?

☑ Have I established rapport with the parents of my most difficult students?

☑ Is there plenty of room for my students to move around in my classroom?

☑ Have I surveyed the students who tend to create problems in class?

☑ Do I know the psychological needs of my students (i.e., why they act as they do)?

☑ Is my instruction in class too difficult or too easy?

☑ Do I structure transitional periods properly and effectively?

☑ Has someone observed me teach to check my discipline strategies?

☑ Do I use time effectively? Do I give enough time breaks to students?

☑ Do I work out of a preventive mode?

☑ Do I set a positive tone in my classroom?

☑ Do I handle most of my discipline problems privately?

☑ Do I appeal to different learning modalities?

☑ Are my lessons brain-compatible?

☑ Do I ask my students to evaluate me on a daily or weekly basis?

Things That Work and Things That Don't Work

As a part of the development of the CLICK program, teachers were surveyed about interventions that work and don't work when it comes to discipline and behavior change. The following two lists reflect the interventions mentioned most often during those interviews. (Interestingly, most of these approaches are the same as those identified by students as tactics that work and don't work.) Feel free to add to these lists for your own use or for use with other educators.

Things That Don't Work

✖ Sending students alone into the hall

✖ Mailing notices of pupil misconduct (Kids intercept the mail.)

✖ Generalized shouting at individual students or groups

✖ Suspending students from school if they are not monitored at home

✖ Using students as office monitors after they are sent to the office for misconduct

✖ Neglecting to report criminal activity of any kind

✖ Scheduling after-school detention at the student's convenience

✖ Failing to follow up on consequences and not setting time lines for improving behavior

✖ Ignoring students breaking school or class rules

✖ Being inconsistent, like favoring certain students over others (e.g., giving athletes or drama students undeserved breaks)

✖ Calling students to the office over the sound system when they have broken school rules

✖ Sending students to the office for minor infractions

✖ Boring instruction

✖ Not having a plan of action in the classroom

✖ Not involving students in establishing rules and consequences

✖ Not setting high expectations

✖ Not establishing a cooperative context in the classroom

✖ Having too many rules for discipline

✖ Getting angry

Things That Work

✔ Establishing trust and rapport with students

✔ Having a definite plan of action

✔ Being consistent and fair

✔ Depriving students of recess

✔ Talking to students about their behavior

✔ Keeping pupils after school for 10 to 15 minutes (Any longer doesn't seem to matter.)

✓ Having a few classroom rules and tying them to teacher expectations

✓ Holding Saturday detention with a teacher or supervisor who knows how to change behavior

✓ Scheduling immediate detention, or within 24 hours of the violation

✓ Requesting that parents sign and return notices about a student's misbehavior, and including a suggestion on what the parents can do to help correct the problem

✓ Having the students write the notes to their parents explaining their misbehavior, and having the notes signed and returned

✓ Sending students who are unruly to another class for a period of time under prearrangement with a cooperating teacher

✓ Promptly calling the police when a criminal violation occurs

✓ Setting up a special class for students who are disruptive that has a social worker or counselor, peer tutors, and a learning specialist (The student is sent there for a specific period of time until the teachers feel he or she can be returned to class.)

✓ Having students carry time cards to be signed by the teachers, attesting to the students' promptness to classes and school (This is checked daily by the assistant principal, principal, ombudsperson, or teacher advisor.)

✓ Insisting that parents come to the school for a meeting when a student's behavior doesn't change; having parents accompany their child throughout the entire school day

✓ Calling in mentors (outside mentors, rather than faculty mentors)

✓ Using the New Behavior Generator (see Chapter 7)

✓ Holding class meetings to discuss with the class when a fellow student constantly violates a rule

✓ Having calm teachers and administrators

✓ Using visual, auditory, and kinesthetic learning strategies

✓ Using incentive cards and rewards for students who perform well; try working out incentives with surrounding businesses or restaurants, for example

✓ Having predictable and consistent classroom routines

✓ Having seating charts

✔ Participating in the CLICK Faculty Meeting (The CLICK Faculty Meeting has proved to be one of the most powerful strategies for improving discipline school-wide.)

✔ Having cheerfully decorated classrooms and schools

✔ Encouraging student involvement

✔ Being proactive

✔ Using student data to determine policies and school rules

✔ Focusing on one major school problem at a time, like truancy, lateness to school, or fights, and truly investigating the problem

✔ Interviewing students regularly about school climate and disciplinary matters

✔ Teaching students problem-solving strategies

✔ Saying "no" when you have to

✔ Finding out the belief behind a student's misbehavior

✔ Providing before-school and after-school tutoring programs

✔ Conducting student CLICK classes

✔ Having designated activity periods that focus on the various interests of students

✔ Arranging community service participation for the students

✔ Providing peer mediation, when required

Chapter 5

The CLICK Faculty Meeting

One way to solve many of your school's discipline problems is through the CLICK Faculty Meeting. This short meeting of faculty members is based on two assumptions: (1) The best way to solve even the most difficult and severe behavioral problems is by utilizing the creative powers of your staff members; and (2) the only way to build consistency in a discipline program is through the sharing of ideas and interventions of all staff members.

Suppose a teacher in the school has had a great deal of trouble with a particular student in terms of behavior. He has tried practically everything in his repertoire of "disciplinary tricks" and has reached out to counselors, administraors, and the child study team. He's at his wit's end, and still the student misbehaves. This is the time for a CLICK Faculty Meeting.

The Process

Step 1   The teacher meets with the faculty and presents the following information to the staff: the age of the student, grade level, the gender of the student, and specifically what the student is doing behaviorally that he hopes to stop. For example, the student enters the classroom yelling and screaming, consistently answers out of turn, is frequently disruptive in class, never listens, and always bothers other students.

Step 2   The facilitator of the CLICK Faculty Meeting (who can be any faculty member, teacher, or administrator) asks, "Of all the behaviors you just mentioned, which one behavior do you want to work on first?" It's important to prioritize and to focus on one behavior because, very often, when one behavioral problem is solved, the other unwanted behaviors resolve as well. Naturally, a teacher wants to curb all of the student's problem behaviors, but trying to address all of them loses focus.

Step 3   After the one behavior is selected, the facilitator elicits a detailed and specific description of that behavior. Continuing with the example given above, "disruptive" and "never listens" are not precise enough. One colleague may think "never listens" means once in a while; another may think that the student really never listens at all (which, of course, is not true). Although the teacher may say "I want her to stop being disruptive," what the teacher really means is "I want her to sit quietly in her seat when I am talking to the class, and not to talk to the person on either side of her."

It's important, therefore, that the teacher be specific in the description of the behavior, breaking it into its smallest possible parts to ensure that everyone knows the exact behavior under discussion. One sure way to obtain a more specific description is to ask the teacher, "If the student were behaving in a way that was acceptable to you, what specifically would she be doing? Describe the behavior to me as if I were watching a movie of the student behaving the proper way."

Step 4   Once the desired behavior is understood, the facilitator breaks the entire group into smaller groups of four to six people each. Their task is to brainstorm creative solutions for solving the presented problem. Of course, the secret to good brainstorming is to think out of the box—to be as creative and unique as possible, without judgment and within reason. If the responses come back as "Prescribe the usual discipline—parent conference, detention, etc.," the facilitator must repeat the brainstorming session until really different and new solutions are generated.

A good example of a creative solution to a discipline problem comes from an actual case. Foreign-born teachers in North Carolina were being trained to teach in U.S. schools. Part of their training included discipline training, and the CLICK Faculty Meeting was introduced to them. In one of the sessions, a teacher presented this problem: She was teaching Spanish in an inner-city high school, and many of the students were using street language and slang. Although she had difficulty understanding them, she knew that they were ridiculing and making fun of her. The problem worsened, and they constantly laughed at her and pointed to her. At the CLICK Faculty Meeting, one of the suggestions was for the teacher to bring a tape recorder into class and to announce to her students that, because she sincerely wished to learn and understand their native language, she was going to record every class and what the students said. She would then take the recorder to the principal, who had agreed to translate for her so that she could join the fun. The laughter, pointing, and ridicule stopped completely. With this creative solution, the teacher avoided what could have been a real disaster if she had confronted the students or threatened them with severe punishment. There was no need for detention, suspensions, confrontations, or arguments.

Step 5   The faculty groups brainstorm for two minutes, and each generates two solutions to the problem. They select a spokesperson, who reads one of the solutions. After hearing each solution, the teacher must tell the group whether she has already tried the offered solution. If so, the facilitator asks for the next solution. This allows the session to go quickly, with no extraneous discussions. When a solution is read that has not been tried, the teacher writes it down and plans to meet with that group after the session to discuss the solution in detail. Each group's solutions are given. In a meeting of 25 to 30 people, it is not unusual to come up with five to 10 very creative solutions. The teacher, then, is equipped with new interventions and should start with the first one the very next day. If it works, fine; if it doesn't work, the teacher goes to the second suggested solution and continues down the list if necessary. If none work, the teacher should call for another CLICK Faculty Meeting, but this is rarely necessary.

The CLICK Faculty Meeting is an effective and powerful tool for teachers:

1. New ideas and solutions are shared to help with discipline in the classroom. Just when teachers feel as if they have no more ideas and the "idea well" has gone dry, they receive 10, 20, 30, or more great interventions.

2. Because all the teachers are sharing these ideas, others in the meeting are also learning new techniques to add to their repertoire of interventions. This builds consistency in the discipline program, and it is especially helpful to new teachers, who very often are at a loss for good disciplinary procedures.

Chapter 6

What Students Need

Much has been said about what students need. Psychology tells us that if some basic needs aren't met, students may run into problems. Interviews with students and teachers on this topic show that *the number one psychological need of both children and teens is the need to be listened to.*

Study on this topic shows there are three more needs students require. They are the need to feel:

◆ Empowered

◆ Connected to someone or something (e.g., a club, sport, etc.)

◆ That they can achieve in school

For students who are considered to be at risk of failure, the need for daily success is critical. This does not mean that the students should be showered with parties or gold stars or medals because they have accomplished an easy task. A simple "Very nice answer on your essay" or "Keep up the good work" will suffice. In other words, praising effort is a good practice.

Of the three basic needs, power and affiliation loom highest. Interviews with students who have engaged in violent behavior reveal that students who do not feel empowered or connected, or both, have a high tendency for violent acts. A student who feels disconnected and powerless will find a way to satisfy his or her rage, as well as his or her need for revenge, attention, and power. The way basic needs affect behavior change will be discussed later in the text.

A brief comment must be made about children and adolescents who may be classified as oppositional or defiant. Such students seem unmanageable either because they are extremely passive and unresponsive or mildly to extremely aggressive. Regardless of attempts to help them, these students don't respond to the usual kinds of discipline. In some cases, they may suffer from a loss of some kind: loss of dignity, loss of respect, loss of a loved one, even loss of a limb. They go through stages of grief for their loss, but not the normal stages. In a normal grieving pattern, one goes through five stages: denial, anger, bargaining, depression, and acceptance.[20] These students seem to follow a different pattern: anger, denial, rage, revenge, and disconnection. When a student who is classified as oppositional or defiant is at any of these stages, traditional interventions will not work. Students who are totally disconnected will not respond to getting in touch with their emotions to change their behavior, or to apologize for something to someone. They usually don't respond to slogans like "Don't Take Drugs!" or "Respect Authority." A more creative approach must be used with these students. One such strategy used in the CLICK program is New Behavior Generator, which is discussed in chapter seven.

A major premise of the CLICK program is that, to really know how to understand behavior, one must have a solid foundation in personality theory. Not all students are alike, and not all students respond to disciplinary directives the same way. For example, detention may work for some students but not others. Conflict resolution works for some, but for others it is meaningless.

So, what do students respond to? They respond to interventions that make sense to them, and to interventions that take into consideration their personalities (including what they value and believe to be important). For example, a student who enjoys the company of others would not make a good candidate for detention hall. Staying after school alone with the teacher makes more sense for such students. A student who wants as little detail as possible would not fare well listening to a lecture from a scolding teacher. Instead of lecturing, the teacher may want to try saying, "This is what I want you to do," and then give one or two sentences of specific instructions. That would most likely give better results.

The CLICK Survey serves several purposes:

◆ It helps teachers to understand themselves and their own behavior.

◆ It helps everyone to appreciate differences in others.

◆ It helps teachers communicate better with students.

---

[20]Kubler-Ross, Elsabeth, *On Death and Dying*. Macmillan Publishing Company (1969); and according to most counseling professionals.

◆ It helps teachers solve discipline problems by pinpointing what a student needs most.

◆ It helps teachers motivate students to change inappropriate behavior by identifying what students value most.

The CLICK Survey lists four categories: Director, Influencer, Stabilizer, and Perfectionist. It must be emphasized that people do not fall into only one of these categories. Each person has certain characteristics from each of the four categories, but there is a core component in each individual that seems dominant. This core component is central to why one acts and reacts in certain ways in given contexts. Call it a core personality; if one tried to act any other way it would feel uncomfortable. For example, a person who likes to do things independently or likes being alone much of the work day could not suddenly work on a continuous basis with large or small groups of people. He or she would be nonproductive in that context after a while. Similarly, when someone is under stress, he or she reverts to the core personality.

STYLE 1
THE DIRECTOR
Goal Oriented
Accepts Challenge
Likes Immediate Results
Makes Quick Decisions
Likes Leading and Taking Control
Direct
Takes Risks and is Daring

DESIRES
Prestige and Authority
Challenges
Varied Activities
Opportunity for Individual Accomplishments

STYLE 2
THE INFLUENCER
People Oriented, Optimistic
Enthusiastic, Motivational
Good Communicator
Good Counselor or Coach
Interactive
Entertaining
Intuitive

DESIRES
Public Recognition
Freedom of Expression
Group Activities
Opportunities to Verbalize

STYLE 3
THE STABILIZER
Consistent, Patient
Likes to Help Others
Loyal
Good Listener
Calms Excited People
Predictable
Task Oriented

DESIRES
Appreciation
Harmonious Environment
Identification with a Group
Credit for Work Accomplished

STYLE 4
THE PERFECTIONIST
Cautious, Analytical
Diplomatic
Pays Attention to Details
Checks for Accuracy
Perfectionist
Critical Thinker
Uses Systematic Approach

DESIRES
Quality and Excellence
Reserved Atmosphere
Details
Opportunity to Demonstrate Expertise

Figure 1. Illustrates the major characteristics and desires. The desires can also be called a person's particular motivations or preferences.

Quick CLICK Survey — *HOW TO RECOGNIZE STYLE*

	DIRECTOR	INFLUENCER	STABILIZER	PERFECTIONIST
Rate of Decision	Very Fast	Fast	Indecisive	Methodical
Emotions	Anger Outburst	Excited Shows Emotion	Hides Feelings	Minimal
Information Needed	Some General	Minimal	Some	Much Detail
Openness	Direct To the point	Very Open and Talkative	Reserved / Limited	Closed / Selective
Conflict	Argumentative	Will Verbalize	Dislikes / Avoids	Will Argue Points or Facts
Hand Gestures	Plenty	Many	Some	Minimal
Activity with Other Students	Selective	A Great Deal	Some	Limited
Note Taking	Minimal	Some	Average	Much
Independence	Very	Some	Little	Somewhat
Control	Angers Easily	Up / Enthusiastic	Supportive	Quiet
Organization	Some	Limited	Organized	Compulsive
Speech	Fast	Talkative	Slow	Very Slow

Figure 2. Lists a number of other factors preferred by each of the personalities labeled as a person's style (how they decide, receive information, speak, etc.). These are only tendencies and hold true in most, but not all, cases. *Style* is just another way to help teachers diagnose a person's tendencies, and how they act, react, and behave.

To illustrate how the profile works, here are a few examples of specific and typical problems teachers encounter, and the suggested interventions to resolve those problems using the CLICK Survey.

DIRECTOR Personality

BASIC NEED —   Power

TENDENCY   —   Defiant, aggressive, or argumentative
                                 (when unruly or under stress)

PROBLEM   —   Teacher starts lecturing and scolding student. Student gets angry and yells and shouts at the teacher, escalating the conflict.

SOLUTION —   Teacher should speak at a fast pace, be direct and assertive, and give the student choices or options to consider to resolve conflict. Should say "What should you be doing?"

INFLUENCER Personality

BASIC NEED —   Affiliation

TENDENCY —   Overly emotional, talkative
                            (when unruly or under stress)

PROBLEM   —   Student is constantly warned about talking to neighbor. Teacher warns student, but student continues to talk.

SOLUTION —   Give student opportunities to verbalize; isolate student; limit group activity as consequence.

STABILIZER Personality

BASIC NEED — Achievement

TENDENCY — Shuts down when (*unruly or under stress*)

PROBLEM — Teacher probably changes activities at a rapid pace; doesn't give student a chance for transition or adaptation.

SOLUTION — Give student a definite plan and give reasons if you change plan.

PERFECTIONIST Personality

BASIC NEED — Achievement

TENDENCY — Argumentative, critical *(when unruly or under stress)*

PROBLEM — Teacher doesn't give the student an opportunity to ask questions or present own information.

SOLUTION — Give student detailed information. Allow student to ask questions.

Personalities in the Extreme

The following are descriptors of the four personalities when they are out of their comfort zone. In other words, each may most likely react in the following manners because of their particular needs and fears.

DIRECTOR — Power hungry, revenge, in your face

INFLUENCER — Outspoken and attention seeking, manipulative

STABILIZER — Desperately seeks group attachments, easily influenced into groups, shuts down, avoidance, feels left out.

PERFECTIONIST — Sneaky, overly critical, relentless

THE QUICK CLICK SURVEY

Instructions: Below, identify those behaviors that are MOST to LEAST characteristic of you in a specific context. Assign 4 points to the characteristic that describes you the most, assign 1 point to the characteristic that describes you the LEAST, 3 points to SECOND MOST, and 2 points in the remaining column. Complete one line at a time. Be sure to have a 1, 2, 3, or 4 on each horizontal line.

ONE		TWO		THREE		FOUR	
GOAL-ORIENTED		ENTHUSIASTIC		STEADFAST		ANALYTICAL	
CONFIDENT		PERSONABLE		PATIENT		CAUTIOUS	
DIRECTING		OPTIMISTIC		SYSTEMATIC		CONSCIENTIOUS	
COMPETITIVE		SPONTANEOUS		EASY GOING		PERFECTIONIST	
DETERMINED		PERSUASIVE		AGREEABLE		CURIOUS	
DARING		IMPULSIVE		STABLE		PRECISE	
RESTLESS		EMOTIONAL		PROTECTIVE		DOUBTING	
COURAGEOUS		CHARMING		ACCOMMODATING		CONSISTENT	
TOTAL		TOTAL		TOTAL		TOTAL	

GRAND TOTAL = 80

After the survey is filled out, add the columns. After that, add the totals across for the four categories. That number should be 80 if your addition is correct. If not, go back and check all the numbers.

Your highest score is your core personality. In some cases there may be two categories that are the same or separated by one or two points. That is normal.

Managing Behavior Through The CLICK Survey

One way to look at behavior is through a student's personality. The CLICK survey gives a teacher important information about personalities. The idea of how this survey can help with interventions is as follows:

The teacher identifies the style of the student (see pg. 43). For example, if the student is unusually talkative, enthusiastic and enjoys a "good time," she obviously would fall under the Influencer category, as opposed to a student who dislikes conflict and change and who likes to help others, a Stabilizer. To further assist the teacher in style, the teacher can refer to pg. 44 for more descriptions.

Once the teacher (or a team of teachers) identifies the personality of the student, the next step is to look at what the student desires most (listed under Desires on pg. 43). Individual interventions should be based on the desires. For example, a Director needs a challenge and a chance to show his or her individual accomplishments. A valid intervention would put the student in charge of a "weaker" student or have the student lead a group with stated goals in mind, since a Director is also goal-oriented.

Thinking creatively about a student's desires can help in the motivation process, and, at the same time, taps into what a student needs most according to his or her personality.

Chapter 7

When a Student Misbehaves: A Suggested Procedure

*W*hen a student misbehaves, it is important for all teachers to have a plan of action, a "what to do when" format. Figure 4 presents suggestions to assist teachers with this procedure, which is particularly helpful for new teachers. This plan or any similar plan that is created must be shared with all faculty members. It should be labeled as a guideline for action.

Figure 4.

What procedure do you follow when a student misbehaves?

See Appendix D, page 73 for full page illustration of Figure 4.

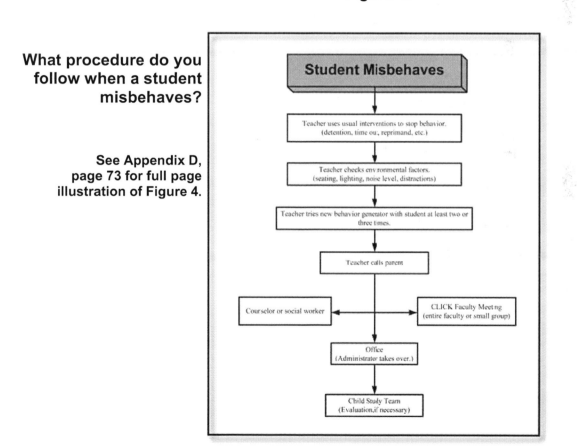

Note: The counselor or social worker can intervene at any level.

Follow the flow chart. If a student misbehaves, the teacher uses the usual interventions to stop the behavior. This includes the typical warnings, contracts, detention, and other traditional kinds of interventions. It is assumed, however, that before these or any interventions are attempted, the teacher has a good idea of the child's personality and has knowledge of what the student generally responds to, rather than guessing about what will work to stop the behavior. If this fails, the teacher checks the environmental factors that might be contributing to or causing the misbehavior. These include seating arrangements, lighting, and learning and teaching styles. If this fails, the teacher, in a one-on-one meeting, tries the New Behavior Generator.

Steps for the New Behavior Generator

This procedure is done one-on-one with a student. First, establish rapport with the student (step 1). Next, ask the student what he or she did (step 2). Sometimes the students really don't know what it was that they did that was considered misbehavior. Once the student knows what he or she did that was wrong, ask the student what rule was violated (step 3). In some cases, students really don't know the rules. The question asked in step 4 helps students think critically and in terms of choice and difference. The question asked in step 5 deals with support the student may need from another student or from a teacher. And the question asked in step 6 encourages the student to verbally commit to the new behavior. Step 7 requires the teacher to actually model the new behavior and then have the student practice the new behavior (sitting, asking politely, etc.).

Teachers should strive for small behavior changes at first. For example, if the student was not sitting in his or her seat when required to do so for any length of time, then have the student practice sitting for just 10 minutes without getting out of his or her seat. Don't require major changes, like expecting the student to sit for 40 minutes without getting up. Less is more in this situation.

After the student has practiced the new behavior, have the student visualize the behavior. Say to the student: "Picture in your mind exactly how you would behave in the future—tomorrow, or next period for example. Pretend you are seeing yourself in a movie and tell me exactly what you are doing, saying, and feeling when you behave this new way."

Have the student do this visualization exercise once or twice, and then ask if this new behavior feels okay. This visualization process imprints the behavior in the student's mind and has proved to be an effective strategy

Finally, if this doesn't work for the student, revise the plan and have the student repeat the process.

The New Behavior Generator Process

1. Establish rapport.

2. What did you do specifically? Get detailed information.

3. What rule did you violate?

4. What can you do differently next time?

5. Do you need any help from anyone?

6. Are you going to do this? (Commitment)

7. Practice, practice, practice. Go for small changes in behavior at first. For example, if a student constantly talks, see if that student is willing to sit quietly for 10 minutes or so. Then, if successful, increase the amount of time to 15 minutes the next time around. Always reward (verbally) positive changes.

8. Make it stick: Have the student visualize the new behavior so that it becomes a more comfortable option for future use.

9. Revise the plan, if necessary.

If the New Behavior Generator does not work, the teacher should call the student's parent or guardian. However, the New Behavior Generator should be used before the phone call, because parents usually ask what you have done so far to try to stop the behavior. Calling too soon may create a problem between the teacher and the parent or guardian, if the parent or guardian feels nothing substantial has been tried by the school.

If parental intervention and awareness doesn't work, the teacher has two other choices, according to this suggested plan: Ask a counselor or social worker to intervene and to provide suggestions to help with problem behaviors, or ask for a CLICK Faculty Meeting.

If ALL of these interventions fail, the last resort would be to ask for administrative assistance or a child study team recommendation. Though this plan has a definite sequence, it is not inflexible. Certainly, a teacher can call a student's home at any time; an administrator or counselor can intervene at any time; and a teacher can use the New Behavior Generator at any time. However, experience in using the suggested sequence contributes to its effectiveness. And, lastly, with minor alterations, the New Behavior Generator can be used as a written contract for a student to carry out.

Chapter 8

Defiant Students and How They Think

Students must be taught how to act. Good behavior is part of a learning process and requires time and effort on both the part of school personnel and the student's parents. Some students, because of a particular disorder or because they haven't been taught to think critically, may have discipline problems. To deal with these students in a logical way, in many cases, is futile. When students, for whatever reason, cannot identify cause and effect, they cannot recognize consequence; students who fail to identify consequence cannot control impulsivity. This leads to disruptive and unwanted behaviors.

Some illustrations of faulty thinking and some ways to challenge and correct faulty thinking are suggested by Neal Bernstein in his book *Treating the Unmanageable Adolescent: A Guide to Oppositional Defiant and Conduct Disorders* (1996).

MINIMIZING THINKING: It's no big deal.

Example: So we all get drunk. What's the big deal? Everybody drinks, and we had a good time.

Challenge: (1) The fact is you're underage and that's illegal. Ever consider that?
(2) So you did it because everyone else drinks. Don't you have a mind of your own? (Reversing)

Example: I stole the kid's bike because he has three of them.

Challenge: You really think it's cool to steal, but you know that's pretty low. Imagine if the bike belonged to your younger sister!

MIND READING: Attributing hostile motives to the actions of others.

Example: He was going to jump me anyway, so I hit him first.

Challenge: **(1)** How could you be so sure he would jump you?
(Checking it out)
(2) You reacted without thinking first. (Confronting)

BLAMING OTHERS

Example: I wouldn't have stolen the beer if the man who works at
the counter didn't go to the bathroom.

Challenge: **(1)** You mean that it's his fault that you stole the beer.
(Reversal)
(2) You chose to steal the beer. The fact is, shoplifting
is a crime. (Confronting)

As the above examples illustrate, sociomoral dilemmas are extremely useful tools for teaching students critical thinking. There are many books available that discuss the use of dilemmas. Teachers can find them in any bookstore, or they can make up their own dilemma scenarios for classroom discussion. The following is one such example from Bernstein:

Theme: Domestic Violence
One night a girl's parents got into a huge argument over money. During the altercation she observed her father (who had been drinking) strike her mother and knock her to the ground. Her mother did not appear hurt but screamed that she would not take this. She proceeded to call 911 and the police were dispatched to the house.

Upon arrival, they asked for the girl's account of what had happened, since she had witnessed the incident. The girl felt close to her father but knew that this was not the first time violence had occurred between her parents. On the other hand, she felt that her mother had always been openly critical of her father and at times provoked his angry reactions. She felt that he was wrong to hit her mother but worried that if charges were pressed, her father might be removed from the home.

After reading this scenario to a class or having the students read it themselves, ask what they would do in this situation. How would they act? What is the best way to think about the situation? The discussion that follows is usually extremely worthwhile and interesting for the students and the teacher.

For elementary teachers, *Raising a Thinking Child* by Myrna B. Shur, Ph.D., is an invaluable resource for teaching kids how to think. The book contains specially designed activities, dialogues, and games. It is also easily adaptable for high school students.

Chapter 9

Teaching Students with Attention Deficit Disorder

Teaching students with attention problems seems to be particularly challenging for teachers. To this point, there are a number of ways not only to keep a student's attention through proper instruction, but there is a specific strategy to incorporate in the lesson plan to guarantee that all the students receive all of the teacher's content and information at the end of each lesson.

The following is the suggested protocol to use for reaching students who have attention problems. It must be noted that this type of lesson plan is successful because it is delivered at a faster pace than usual to keep the attention of all the students (in many instances, slowing down or waiting for a student will cause the other students to become impatient or rambunctious), and the teacher should use a system of "overlapping" or reviewing of each previous step to ensure that students receive all the information, in case they didn't when the information or content was first presented.

**Lesson Plan
(Students Grouped in Pairs)**

1. The teacher asks a profound or extremely interesting question: "How do we remember things? What goes on in our brains?"

2. The teacher then asks each student to write a response to that question. At this point the teacher scans the room, and when he notices that one or two students have finished, he says, "Please put your pens down and tell your partner what you wrote. It's okay if you haven't finished; just tell the person what you intended to write. (30-40 seconds)

3. When the students are finished discussing, the teacher lectures on how the brain remembers. (5 minutes)

4. After the lecture, the teacher asks the students to write down briefly what new things they learned about the subject. Again, the teacher

scans the room and when one and or two students have finished writing, the teacher asks all the students to stop writing and elicits responses from four or five students, who respond out loud.

5. Next, the teacher tells the class that he is going to demonstrate how the students can improve their memory using a number of mind tricks. (10 minutes)

6. After the demonstration, all the students pair up and practice various memory strategies and test each other's "new-and-improved" memories. (10 minutes)

7. The teacher then stops the activity and tells the students to write what they learned from this activity and share their responses with the group next to them.

8. The teacher then asks the students to write an outcome sentence that can also serve as an evaluation statement (I was surprised...I learned...I wonder...I think...).

9. Students with similar outcomes can be paired for further study or research that leads into a new unit of study for the group.

Lesson Plan 2

1. The teacher shows a short film clip.

2. Students in pre-assigned groups, discuss what they viewed and come up with a one-word response.

3. Teacher briefly comments on students responses. (5 minutes).

4. Teacher explains film clip.

5. Teacher demonstrates concept, idea, skill from film.

6. Students practice what the teacher demonstrated to them.

7. Student groups report results of their practice.

8. Students fill in the outcome sentence (I will…)

9. Teacher groups students with common outcomes for further study. Remember, the above lesson can be varied and adapted into many forms and plans. For example, the teacher can start the lesson with a provocative saying, film clip, joke, work of art, choral reading, or any other novel activity. The secret is to keep the students sharing and pairing, and review continuously. Notice that this type of lesson contains all the necessary ingredients for effective learning.[21]

---

[21] Note: The above lesson format has been adapted from the standard training lessons used by the Eastern NLP Institute, Newtown, Pennsylvania. We have shortened the lecture time considerably for our purposes. In addition, the idea of working at an accelerated pace comes from the author's experience working with students who have ADD and neurofeedback disorders. (See *Getting Rid of Ritalin*, Hill and Castro.)

Chapter 10

Intervention Plan

*T*raditional behavioral interventions fail with many students. In most schools, behavior modification is the norm for handling most disciplinary matters. Yet, behavior modification is only effective for about 1% of the student population. When an intervention is targeted at the same level that it occurs, nothing happens. Problems generally are solved by elevating the intervention to a value or belief level, or through behavior shaping by connecting a value to the new behavior.

In some cases, beliefs can be changed by completely altering behavior through continuous experience of a new behavior in small steps until an individual feels comfortable with the behavior (the New Behavior Generator). In this instance, using sensory modalities (visual, auditory, and kinesthetic) must be integrated into the student's mind through a visualization process.

Below is a recommended procedure to follow for changing an unwanted behavior to an acceptable behavior. Notice that the steps do not follow the traditional guidelines that teachers, counselors, administrators, or child study teams use in schools. Compare the method to the usual interventions used in schools and one thing glaringly stands out. In traditional interventions the student who is trying to be helped finds himself or herself going back and forth, from inside the school to the outside of the school, with little results for change in behavior. For example, the student may first find himself or herself in detention for misbehavior (inside the school); the next step might require a call home (outside the school); the next, a parent conference or conference with a counselor (inside the school); the next, suspension (outside the school); the next, a parent conference (inside); the next, a therapist (outside); and so on.

This sort of bouncing back and forth is all too common. Here is a more comprehensive approach to solving disciplinary problems.

Step-by-Step Intervention Process

1. Gain rapport with the student.

2. Determine the student's learning style (e.g., visual, auditory, kinesthetic).

3. Determine the student's personality style (use the CLICK Survey).

4. Identify the student's chief motivator (e.g., power, affiliation, achievement).

5. Identify the student's highest personal values or beliefs (use the CLICK Survey).

6. Try using the New Behavior Generator to achieve behavioral change.

7. Conduct a CLICK Faculty Meeting (for creative solutions to the problems).

8. Create and connect specific intervention to the student's values and belief system.

9. Refer to administrator or counselors; refer to child study team.

10. Seek advice from others: e.g., mentors, peer coaches, CLICK Room* staff.

* The CLICK Room: This is a special room in a school that has been designated for working with students who have behavioral problems. The special room has a social worker, learning specialist, and peer tutors who all work one-on-one with the identified student(s) for as long as it takes for the student(s) to be placed back into their regular program.

Conclusion

---

*A*s teachers and administrators, we sometimes forget what it was like growing up. It's a difficult process. Today's children face a vast array of new challenges, difficulties and responsibilities. Sometimes it's a painful journey; sometimes not. We often find many children saying through their actions and misdeeds, "Please help me. I don't know what to do or how to act!" As was said previously, most discipline issues are cries for help.

The CLICK program encourages kids to be responsible, to think about the choices they make about their behavior, and to appreciate differences among people. Talking to students is critical to learning about their behavior; so the CLICK program encourages teachers to be curious about the way students behave. Don't get mad at the behavior if you don't agree with it. Instead, ask yourself, "I wonder what is going on in that student's mind that is causing that behavior." Then, talk to that student and lead him/her to a better place.

There's an old metaphor to sum up what I am trying to convey to educators about discipline that also has implications for teaching in general. The passage below is adapted from David Gordon's book <u>Therapeutic Metaphors</u>.

A young boy was walking home from school one day, when he came upon a runaway horse. The boy knew he needed to return the horse to its owner. After settling the horse down, he gently mounted the horse, took the reins, and said, "Giddy-up!'" The horse headed straight for the main road.

Trotting along, the horse continued in what seemed like the "right" direction. Every so often, the boy would lightly tug at the reins keeping the horse on the path of the main road. About four or five miles down the road, the horse turned into a small farm where the farmer called out to him saying, "Hey, boy! Over here! Where did you find my horse?"

The young boy shouted back, "A few miles down the road!"

"How did you know it was my horse and how did you know to come here?" the farmer asked.

"I didn't know," said the boy. "The <u>horse</u> knew. All I did was to keep his attention on the road."

This is the way to guide students to better behavior!

APPENDIX A

HOW TO SET UP A CLASSROOM

Physical space has a bearing on effective discipline. It is best for teachers to be able to view all of their students from any one spot in the classroom. In addition, arranging desks in the classroom in a strategic manner helps with discussion, physical movement, collaboration, and other such matters.

Below are highly recommended seating arrangements for teachers.

Example 1

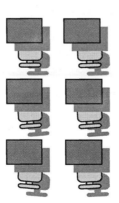

Example 2

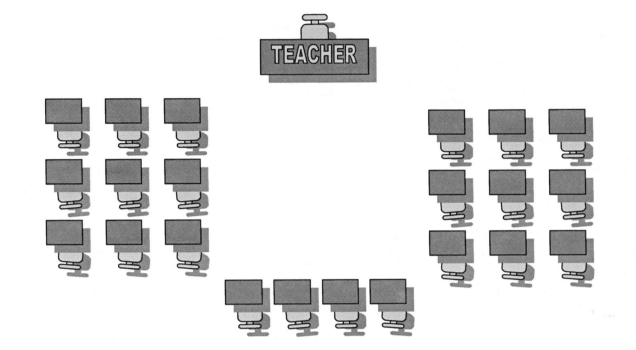

Example 3

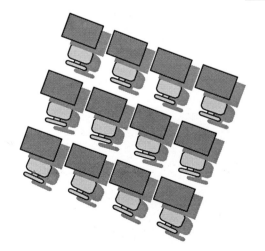

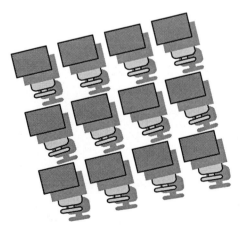

Example 4

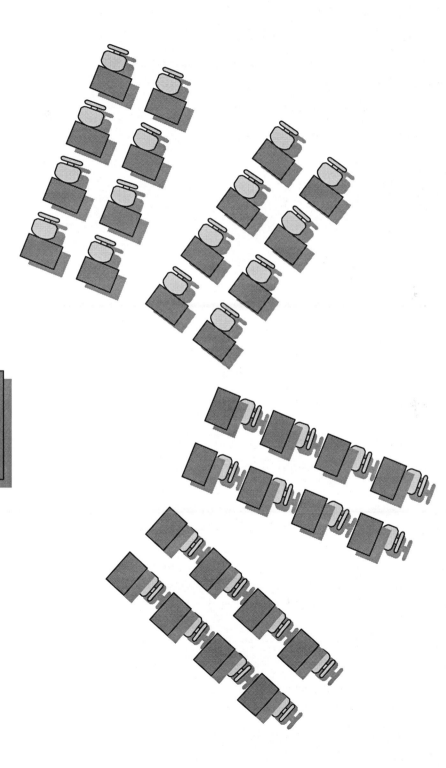

Example 5

Example 6

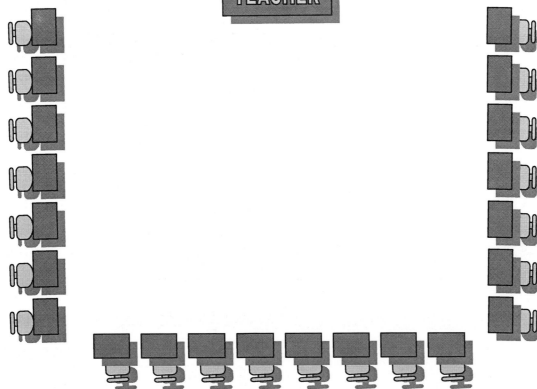

Example 7

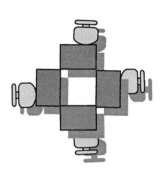

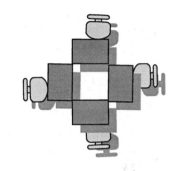

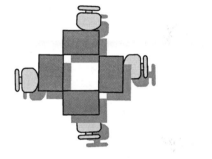

APPENDIX B

MATCHING INSTRUCTIONAL STRATEGIES

A good way to understand the four personality types identified in the CLICK Survey is to match instructional strategies with the personality type. On the list below, indicate the personality type that would best prefer the listed strategy. Indicate by writing a D, I, S, or P in the space provided by each number (see page 71 for answer key).

_____1. **BEHAVIOR MODELING** – A technique in which behavior is demonstrated to students. Then the students practice the behavior with guidance and feedback.

_____2. **CASE STUDY** – A written account of a situation is presented to students. Students are asked, either individually or in a small group, to analyze the case and present recommendations.

_____3. **COMPUTER BASED TRAINING** – Students receive information and instruction, then responds, and receives feedback via interaction with a computer.

_____4. **CRITIQUE** – Students analyze topics, systems, processes, etc., assess strengths and weaknesses, then make suggestions for improvement.

_____5. **DEMONSTRATION** - Students observe a performance. The demonstration may be live or recorded.

_____6. **DISCUSSION** – An open exchange of ideas on a topic. Discussions may be unstructured or highly structured, leaderless or moderated.

_____7. **DRILL** - Repetitive practice session designed to increase efficiency or aid retention.

_____8. **FIELD TRIP** – Students participate in an educational opportunity off campus.

_____9. **IN-BASKET** – A case study in which items are presented to students as an in-basket. Students must prioritize, make decisions and solve problems

_____10. **JOB AIDS** – A procedural guide that provides step-by-step instructions on the job. Types of job aids are: worksheets; decision tables; flow charts; manuals; checklists; etc.

_____11. **LECTURE** – A teacher prepares and delivers a lengthy oral presentation.

_____12. **LECTURETTE** – A brief oral presentation by a presenter.

_____13. **MENTAL IMAGERY** –Students visualize images, ideas and concepts in their heads.

_____14. **SIMULATION** – Students practice a task which simulates real-job situations.

_____15. **TEAM TEACHING** – Two or more instructors present training.

MATCHING INSTRUCTIONAL STRATEGIES

ANSWER KEY FOR

S 1. **BEHAVIOR MODELING** – A technique in which behavior is demonstrated to students. Then the students practice the behavior with guidance and feedback.

P 2. **CASE STUDY** – A written or oral account of a situation is presented to students. Students are asked, either individually or in a small group, to analyze the case and present recommendations.

P 3. **COMPUTER BASED TRAINING** – Students receive information and instruction, then responds, and receives feedback via interaction with a computer.

P 4. **CRITIQUE** – Students analyze topics, systems, processes, etc., assess strengths and weaknesses, then make suggestions for improvement.

S 5. **DEMONSTRATION** - Students observe a performance. The demonstration may be live or recorded.

I 6. **DISCUSSION** – An open exchange of ideas on a topic. Discussions may be unstructured or highly structured, leaderless or moderated.

S 7. **DRILL** - Repetitive practice session designed to increase efficiency or aid retention.

D,I,S,P 8. **FIELD TRIP** Students participate in an educational opportunity off campus.

D 9. **IN-BASKET** – A case study in which items are presented to students as an in-basket. Students must prioritize, make decisions and solve problems.

S 10. **JOB AIDS** – A procedural guide that provides step-by-step instructions on the job. Types of job aids are: worksheets; decision tables; flow charts; manuals; checklists; etc.

I 11. **LECTURE** – A teacher prepares and delivers a lengthy oral presentation.

D 12. **LECTURETTE** – A brief oral presentation by a presenter.

I 13. **MENTAL IMAGERY** –Students visualize images, ideas and concepts in their heads.

S 14. **SIMULATION** – Students practice a task which simulates real-job situations.

I,S 15. **TEAM TEACHING** – Two or more instructors present training.

APPENDIX C

BASIC COMMUNICATION PATTERNS IN CLICK

It is recommended that responses to disruptive students be kept at a minimum, but that these responses have leverage.

Below are the five patterns that work in many instances involving conflict and defiance.

Communication Pattern One
    A. **Computer Mode** –Respond by saying, "Regardless" as demonstrated in the text.
    B. Used in an exchange to keep a child focused on the real problem or issue, it also helps to avoid endless arguments and power struggles.

Communication Pattern Two
    A. **The Allusion of Choice** – "You can either carry your jackets outside or put them on now." *(The goal here is to get the children to take their jackets.* You can:
       1. Whisper or talk quietly.
       2. Turn in assignments now or at the end of class.
       3. Answer questions aloud or on paper.
       4. Read the book on the floor or at your desk.
       5. Study with a friend or by yourself.
    B. The cases above are used to give the student the allusion of choice. However, the end result has already been determined by the teacher.

Communication Pattern Three
    A. **Redirecting** – "What should you be doing?" instead of "What are you doing?" "John, I like the way you are working, and that will result in a good project." *(Said in the direction of another student who is off task.)*
    B. Used to direct behavior toward a positive goal.

Communication Pattern Four
    A. **Reflection** – "O.K., you violated the rule. What do you suppose I can do to you now?" The student responds by saying, "You can give me detention or call my parents."
    B. Used to get kids to think about consequences and problem solve.

Communication Pattern Five
    A. **Praise Phrase** – "Just because I like you, do you think I should let you continue to do this?"
    B. Used to slightly confuse the student, but switching his or her internal state quickly through praise.

APPENDIX D

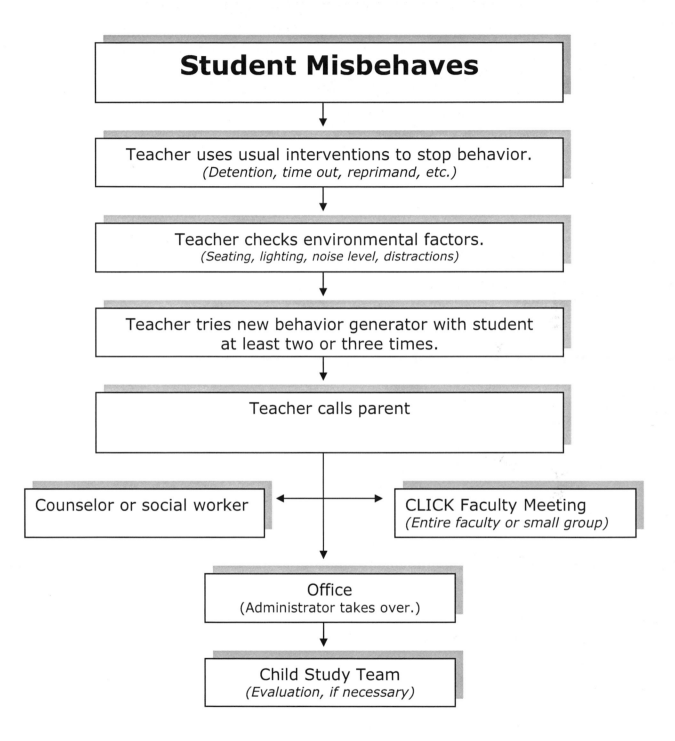

Student Misbehaves

Teacher uses usual interventions to stop behavior.
(Detention, time out, reprimand, etc.)

Teacher checks environmental factors.
(Seating, lighting, noise level, distractions)

Teacher tries new behavior generator with student at least two or three times.

Teacher calls parent

Counselor or social worker

CLICK Faculty Meeting
(Entire faculty or small group)

Office
(Administrator takes over.)

Child Study Team
(Evaluation, if necessary)

Figure 4.

Note: The counselor or social worker can intervene at any level.

RESOURCES

Ashby, W., *An Introduction to Cybernetics*, Wiley, (1957).

Bandler, R. and Grinder, J., *The Structure of Magic*, Palo Alto, CA, Science and Behavior Books, Inc. (1975).

Blackerby, D., *Rediscover the Joy of Leading*, Success Skills, Inc., Oklahoma City, OK (1996).

Blankstein, A., *Lessons for Life: How Smart Schools Boost Academic, Social, and Emotional Intelligence*, (2003). In M.J. Elias, H. Arnold, and C. Stieger-Hussey (Ed.Ds.). *EQ &IQ: Best Leadership Practices for Caring and Successful Schools*, Thousand Oaks, CA, Corwin Press.

Bodenhammer, Gregory, *Back In Control: How To Get Children To Behave*, Fireside, New York, NY (1992).

Costa, Arthur, and Garmston, Robert, *Cognitive Coaching*, Norwood, MA, Christopher-Gordon Publishers, (1994).

DePorter, Bobbi with Hernacki, Mike, *Quantum Learning*, Dell Publishing, (1992).

Dilts, R., *Applications of Neuro-Linguistic Programming; A Practice to Communications Learning and Change*, Meta Publications, Cupertino, CA, (1983).

Dilts, Robert, *Dynamic Learning*, Meta Publications, Capitola, CA (1995).

Feurstein, Reuven, *Instrumental Enrichment: An Intervention Program for Cognitive Modifiability*, Scott, Foresman and Co., Glenview, IL (1980).

Gordon, David, *Therapeutic Metaphors*, Meta Publications, Capitola, CA (1978).

Jensen, E., Brain-*Based Learning*, 2nd Edition, San Diego, CA The Brain Store (2000).

Kohn, Alfie, *Beyond Discipline: From Compliance to Community*, Association for Supervision and Curriculum Development, Alexandria, Virginia, ASCD Publishers (1996).

Kubler-Ross, Elsabeth, *On Death and Dying*, Macmillan Publishing Company (1969); and according to most counseling professionals.

Levy, Ray and O'Hanlon, Bill, *Try and Make Me: Simple Strategies That Turn Off the Tantrums and Create Cooperation*, Rodale Inc. (2002).

Payne, Ruby K., *A Framework For Understanding Poverty* (Third Revised Edition), Aha! Process, Inc. (2003).

Saphier, Jon, and Grower, Robert, *The Skillful Teacher*, 5th Edition, Research for Better Teaching, Inc., Carlisle, MA (1997).

Scannella, A. and Webster-O'Dell, Wendi (Eds.), *The Children We Share*, the Foundation for Educational Administration and the New Jersey Principals and Supervisors Association, Monroe Twp. NJ, funded by the New Jersey Department of Education, (2003).

Shure, Myrna, Ph.D., *Raising a Thinking Child*, Simon and Schuster Inc. (1994).

Sousa, D., *How the Brain Learns: A Classroom Teacher's Guide*, 2nd Edition, Thousand Oaks, CA, (2001).

The Quick CLICK Survey, Hecht, D., New Jersey Principals and Supervisors Association, (1996).

HIGHLY SUGGESTED READING

Hill, Robert, Ph.D. and Castro, Eduardo, M.D., ***Getting Rid of Ritalin***, Hampton Roads Publishing Company, Inc., Charlottesville, VA (2002).

Kohn, Alfie, ***Beyond Discipline, from Compliance to Community***, ASCD, Alexandria, VA (1996).

Nelson, Linda and Lott, Lynn, ***Positive Discipline for Teenagers***, Pima Publishing, Rocklin, CA (1994).

Taffel, Ron, ***Getting Through to Difficult Kids and Parents, Uncommon Sense for Child Professionals***, The Guilford Press, New York and London (2001).

Levy, Ray Ph. D.and O'Hanlon, Bill M.S., L.M.F.T. with Goode, Tyler Norris, ***Try and Make Me! Simple Strategies That Turn Off the Tantrums and Create Cooperation***, Rodale, Inc. USA (2001).

SUGGESTED ORGANIZATIONS AND WEBSITES FOR PERSONAL RESEARCH

Educational Research Service
2000 Clarendon Boulevard
Arlington, Virginia 22201-2908

(703) 243-2100 phone
(703) 243-1985 fax
www.ers.org

National Education Association
1201 16th Street, NW
Washington, DC 20036-3290

(202) 833-4000 phone
(202) 822-7974 fax
www.nea.org

Families and Advocates Partnership for
Education (FAPE) Coordinating Office
PACER Center
8161 Normandale Boulevard
Minneapolis, MN 55437-1044

(952) 838-9000 phone
(952) 838-1099 fax
www.fape.org

NY Civil Liberties Union
125 Broad Street
New York, NY   10004

(212) 344-3005 phone
(212) 344-3318 fax
www.nyclu.org

The Council for Exceptional Children (CEC)
1110 North Glebe Road, Suite 300
Arlington, VA 22201

(703) 620-3660 voice phone
(866) 915-5000 phone
(703) 264-9494 fax
www.eircec.sped.org

Teacher/Pathfinder, an educational internet village   www.teacherpathfinder.org

Regional Educational Laboratories   www.relnetwork.org

About the Author

Dr. Anthony Scannella

Dr. Anthony Scannella is presently Chief Executive Officer of the Foundation for Educational Administration, Inc. (FEA). Prior to this, Dr. Scannella served as a successful principal, assistant principal, director of curriculum and teacher. He is the author/co-author of a number of notable projects including *Reading into Writing*, part of a nationally-validated writing project for schools; *Sending the Right Signals*, a program to eliminate sexual harassment; and co-author of *The Children We Share*, a program for parents and principals. He has trained at the state, national and international levels. Dr. Scannella received his doctorate from Rutgers University and was awarded the Distinguished Educator Award from the Rutgers Graduate School of Education for outstanding and exemplary service in his field.

Dr. Scannella can be reached at 1 (609) 860-1200 or by email at ascannella@njpsa.org.